Māori Animal Myths
Mōkai Rangatira

Warren Pohatu

The Children of Tane and Tangaroa

Every living creature descends from Ranginui (the sky father) and Papatuanuku (the earth mother). Rangi and Papa had a number of sons including Tane-Mahuta (god of the forests) and Tangaroa (god of the sea). All land-based animals like birds, rats, dogs and even humans trace their descent from Tane. All the creatures of the sea, reptiles and insects trace their descent from Tangaroa. Therefore we are all children of Rangi and Papa and we are all related to each other like one big family.

This is why Maori believe all creatures great and small are brothers and sisters. Most animals are, in fact, our older siblings as most were created long before humans arrived. This shared whakapapa (genealogy) makes humans' relationship with the animal kingdom rather complex. While humans respects these creatures they also have a desire to dominate them. Humans are willing to respect animals yet they would not hesitate to eat them either.

Early Maori acquired a taste for almost every mammal, fish and plant within their realm and developed a thorough understanding of the environment they lived in and the creatures who shared it with them. Every opportunity to nourish and sustain themselves was taken and nothing went to waste. Whatever could be used would be used.

Humans' spiritual bond with creatures like the whale and the dolphin could never override a basic need for food. The first priority was survival yet despite being in such a compromising position, many ancestors managed to forge special bonds with the animal kingdom. The following are a few examples of those special relationships with special animals. Toitu te mana o nga matua!

Whale

The whale has always been an important member of our family. The whale is definitely the biggest big brother anyone can have. As the largest of Tangaroa's children it has been revered by every generation of Maori since time began. When the earliest explorers left their homelands to travel to Aotearoa they made sure to bring everything that was important to them. Amongst these treasured possessions was the mauri or life forces of the various creatures, places and objects.

Ruawharo is said to have brought the mauri of the whales on board the Takitimu canoe. This mauri was in the form of special rocks taken from a sacred pool in Hawaiki. When he arrived here he placed the rocks at various points and thus established a sacred life-force for the local whale population.

Apart from the special spiritual bond between humans and whales there was also a very practical bond. The whale provided early Maori with store-houses full of provisions. There was meat for food, oil for burning, bone for weapons, and teeth for special ornaments. The whale, either dead or alive, was a real treasure to the Maori. Maori did not differentiate between the two. They believe that where one life ends another begins.

Of course some of our most famous ancestors had a special bond with the whales. On the east coast of the North Island Paikea is one such ancestor. Paikea was on board a canoe called Tutepewarangi when his brother Ruatapu, in a fit of jealousy, capsized the canoe then tried to kill everyone on board. Paikea called to his ancestors to help and a whale soon appeared to whisk him away to safety. Paikea, the whale rider, eventually settled on the east coast at a place called Whangara-mai-Tawhiti and is a very important ancestor of Ngati Porou people.

Dolphin

The children of Tangaroa celebrate the joys of life with such passion but none celebrate with more energy or flair than the dolphin. The dolphins' playful antics have earned them a reputation as special guardians. To see them escorting canoes was a good omen, as if Tangaroa himself had endorsed the journey with a guard of honour. Playful dolphins were more often nominated as kaitieke (guardians) rather than taniwha (monsters).

Like most creatures of the sea they were often used as food. Early Maori believed that beached whales or dolphins were a gift from Tangaroa. It would be insulting not to accept or make good use of this gift because Tangaroa's sacrifice was far too great to ignore. Most coastal tribes ate dolphin meat. They also used the oil and bone because, in Maori society, nothing was ever wasted.

Early explorers always had guardians of some kind. Kupe's guardian is said to have been a white dolphin called Tuhirangi. When Kupe set out from Rarotonga in pursuit of a giant octopus that had been stealing bait, Tuhirangi escorted him. Kupe found the octopus at Raukawa (Cook Strait) and after a great battle he killed the fierce monster. He then returned to his homeland to tell them of the new land he had discovered. He left Tuhirangi, his white dolphin, as a guardian of the area. Tuhirangi now lives there in a cave called Kaikaiawaro. His task is to guide craft safely through the treacherous waters around Te Au-miti (French Pass).

In the early 1900s a white dolphin was often seen around French Pass, skipping across the bow wave of boats in the area. So frequent was its appearance that it was given a name — Pelorus Jack. However, local Maori believe that this was actually Kupe's white dolphin, Tuhirangi.

Shark

Shark is the strong silent type and is feared in Maori culture as much as he is in any other. His hard-earned reputation as a streamlined killing machine is quite universal. Shark is Tangaroa's fiercest warrior and when in his own element he is far too potent for even the bravest men. However, despite humans' respect for the shark's prowess as a warrior, it was still a favourite food and was hunted all along the coastline.

In the east dried shark was a favourite amongst the old people. Today it is still prepared in the traditional manner and is still very much a delicacy. The flesh is cut into strips then dried in the sun for a week. It lasts indefinitely and tastes great.

Many coastal tribes have sharks as guardians. One such tribe is Ngai Tamanuhiri of the East Coast. Their guardian is called Moremore and is described as a shark with no tail. Moremore patrols the rugged coast between Te Muriwai and Nukutaurua. He is not dangerous himself but warns locals of danger.

Another East Coast ancestor called Mahaki-rau had a pet shark called Ikahoea. Mahaki-rau had heard of an underwater tree so he sent Ikahoea to the depths of the ocean to fetch a branch. He then planted that branch and it grew into the kahikatea. The large forests of kahikatea grow well in areas surrounded by water such as swamps and marshlands.

One of the best known kowhaiwhai patterns takes its name from the shark family. Mangopare (hammerhead shark) is a pattern used a lot on the East Coast. The Mangopare symbolised speed and strength. His eyes move independently of each other, which allows him to see both sides at once. That makes our brother Mangopare a born diplomat!

Seal

The seal is by far the most laid-back member of our extended family, perhaps a little too laid-back. Seals were an important food source of the early Maori. When our ancestors arrived the seal colonies were vast and numerous. Not only was the meat consumed but the blubber and skin were useful as well. Seals are another of Tangaroa's special children. Blessed with grace, speed and agility in the deep blue oceans, seals can also emerge from the water to be comfortable on land. That means seals have the power to link the realms of fish and humans.

Ngake accompanied Kupe in his quest to kill the great octopus of Muturangi. After a battle at Raukawa (Cook Strait) Kupe returned to Rarotonga. Ngake and his wife Hinewaihua stayed behind to explore the strange new land called Aotearoa.

They explored the southern coast and found many new creatures like seals and penguins. Hinewaihua was mesmerised by the new creatures and she adopted them as pets. When it was time to return home she was reluctant to leave them behind. But her husband told her that because there were no people around, her creatures were quite safe. So Hinewaihua left her pets in the cold regions of the South Island where they still thrive today.

An ancestor called Te Wera was a famous Ngai Tahu warrior. He was a ruthless fighting chief who knew no fear in battle. On one excursion to Rakiura (Stewart Island) Te Wera lead his men into battle. They easily defeated the local tribe. Then as Te Wera ran along a beach he was confronted by a two-tonne bull sealion. Having never seen one before Te Wera turned and run. So it is said that Te Wera finally met his match.

Eel

Most families have a sly, untrustworthy member and eel is the sly, sneaky member in our family. But despite such an unsavoury reputation eel was certainly an important part of Maori history. Eels are the most prolific freshwater fish available in Aotearoa. Maori became expert at catching them, developing various traps to do so. Along the bigger rivers eel weirs were as important as bird hunting grounds. They were protected with passion by locals.

A number of taniwha took the form of the eel and the greatest of them all was the father of the eels called Tuna-roa. He was a giant who lived near the home of Maui and his wife Hinauri. Every day Hinauri would bath in a stream near the swamp. One day Tuna-roa spied her there and slithered unnoticed into her pool. As Hinauri got up to leave Tuna-roa burst forth and knocked her down. He slithered over her body, eventually seducing her. Hinauri was too ashamed to tell Maui. The next day she returned as usual to her pool. Tuna-roa knocked her down and again had his way with her. This time Hinauri went straight to her husband and told him. Maui was furious.

He dug a channel from the swamp to the ocean, damming it at the swamp end. Maui stretched a net across the channel, then sat down to pray for rain. Soon it was raining so hard the swamp began to flood. Maui removed the dam. The waters rushed from the swamp to the ocean, dragging Tuna-roa into Maui's net. Maui jumped down and cut the eel into pieces. The head was removed and sank into the sea becoming a fish. The tail was hacked off and dropped into the waves to become conger eel. The body was cut into many pieces, which slithered into the swamp where they became the multitudes of freshwater eels found today.

Octopus

Our brother the octopus has a rather sinister reputation due to his odd appearance. Yet when in his natural element the octopus is gracefully intelligent and represents the wisdom of Tangaroa. His ability to camouflage himself is testimony to his brilliance. Despite its odd look the octopus is a favourite food of the Maori. They were caught around the coast and were a delicacy.

Long ago in Rarotonga a great tohunga called Muturangi lived in a small village near the sea. He had a pet octopus and allowed the beast to roam freely in the ocean. Kupe also lived in that village. He set his long-line off the coast every day. After a while the greedy octopus began to steal bait from Kupe's lines. Then as the octopus grew bolder, it began stealing all the bait from all the lines leaving nothing for Kupe and the other fishermen.

Kupe was furious when he learnt about the antics of the octopus and he vowed to kill the pest. He launched his canoe Matahourua and gave chase. The octopus sped across the ocean eventually arriving at Raukawa (Cook Strait). Kupe caught up with the beast and they fought a great battle. Then with one almighty blow Kupe killed it.

After the beast died Kupe cut out its eyes placing them at a spot called Nga Whatu (the Eyes). Its English name is The Brothers. Kupe then hacked off its legs and cut the body into pieces. The battle had been so fierce it shredded the landscape.

When Kupe finally took time to look around he realised he had found a strange new land. It was huge with lush bush and bountiful oceans. Kupe quickly explored it then returned to Rarotonga to tell of his discovery. In time he would return to begin the Maori migration to Aotearoa.

Stingray

Stingray is a descendant of Punga, son of Tangaroa. Punga is acknowledged as the father of ugly creatures. Stingrays, sharks, reptiles and insects are all considered to be children of Punga. Despite their ugly tag stingrays glide gracefully through the water like birds through the sky, yet when they need to hide they simply merge with their surroundings. Stingrays often patrol river mouths in search of food, making these places dangerous to any fishermen trawling in the area.

The stingray has a poisonous barb at the base of his tail and if he is accidentally stood on he can deliver a painful and sometimes lethal blow. This has earned the stingray a reputation as a nasty, foul-tempered beast. Despite this, stingray was a very tasty meal for the early Maori. They were easily caught and were plentiful in almost all areas.

Several ancestors brought or adopted stingrays as kaitieki. One such ancestor was Paoa, the captain of Horouta canoe. As he travelled along the East Coast he left these kaitieki at various points. Just off Matakaoa is a flat rock called Te Whai-o-Paoa (The Stingray of Paoa). It still sits there today watching over the local coastline.

Some Maori believe the stingray played a major role in our culture long before any of the canoes arrived. In fact when Maui hauled up the great fish which eventually became the North Island, that fish was said to be a giant stingray. When you next look at a map of the North Island imagine the East Coast as one wing, the west coast as the other while the far north is its tail and Wellington the head.

Gecko

Despite his small size and cute appearance, gecko terrified early Maori settlers. Reptiles are the children of Punga, a son of Tangaroa. Punga is known as the father of ugly creatures like stingrays, sharks, reptiles and insects. Punga had two sons called Ika-tere and Tu-tewehiwehi. When Tawhirimatea (god of the winds) attacked Tangaroa (god of the sea) it caused chaos amongst the sea god's many descendants. Ika-tere fled below the waves and became an ancestor of the fish while Tu-tewehiwehi hid on shore becoming the ancestor of reptiles.

All lizards are the children of Moko-hiku-waru, a giant reptile god that lived in the Taranaki area. Moko-hiku-waru and another giant reptile called Tu-tangata-kino are said to be guardians of the house of Miru, ruler of the underworld. Both were very dangerous creatures. Special tohunga could employ these giant reptiles to attack their enemies or guard special objects or places. It was common to employ the descendants of Moko-hiku-waru, like the gecko, to guard hidden treasures and family heirlooms.

Another reptile god called Te Ngangara-huarau lived near Rangitoto (D'Urville Island). One day the monster kidnapped a woman from a nearby village. He took the woman back to his cave where he made her his wife. The woman managed to escape and returned to her village. When she told her brothers about her ordeal they decided to capture and kill the beast.

The brothers built a strong house to hold the giant. They lured it to their village using their sister as bait. When they finally got him inside they slammed the door shut then set the house on fire. The giant reptile died in the flames and the people were safe at last.

Kiwi

Undoubtedly one of the most important members of our family, the kiwi represents the soul of Tane-Mahuta and lives in the heart of the forest. Like the heart, the kiwi remains largely unseen yet without it the forest would simply die. Maori have always treasured the kiwi. Its feathers are prized by cloak makers all over the country and there is no finer cloak than a korowai-kiwi (kiwi cloak).

On the East Coast a chief named Rongokako had a giant pet kiwi. The bird was so big that it could not be killed by humans. Rongokako was the son of Tamatea-Arikinui, captain of Takitimu, and they lived around Heretaunga (Hawkes Bay). Paoa captained the Horouta canoe and lived at Turanga (Gisborne).

For some reason these two became rivals. Paoa challenged Rongokako to a race from the East Coast to the far north. Rongokako accepted the challenge and the race started at Heretaunga. Paoa boarded his canoe and sailed up the coast. When he reached Uawa he heard Rongokako was coming overland riding his giant kiwi. Its strides were huge, clearing mountain tops in one step. Paoa decide to stop the kiwi.

Somewhere between Waipiro and Tokomaru Paoa built a huge trap to catch the giant bird. As Rongokako approached on his kiwi he noticed something strange about the path. He saw the trap and was able to deal it a mighty blow with his taiaha. The trap sprung with such force that it flew into the air. The place where the trap finally landed is now known as Mount Arowhana. The place where Paoa set his trap is called Te Tawhiti-o-Rongokako (The trap of Rongokako). Rongokako and his kiwi went on with the race. Paoa was so shocked he never did manage to catch them and so Rongokako won.

Dog

We've always had dogs in our families and what's more they've always been considered our best friend. Dogs arrived with their masters on the canoes and were used as hunting partners, guards and companions. Many others were raised for food, as red meat was extremely scarce. Apart from the meat, the skin was highly valued for cloak making.

Most animals descended from the realm of gods but dogs owe their existence to Maui. One day, Maui went fishing with his sister's husband Irawaru. Despite taking his special hook, carved from his grandmother's jawbone, Maui caught no fish. On the other hand Irawaru caught fish after fish, almost filling the canoe with tamure and hapuka.

Maui could barely hide his anger. Secretly he suspected Irawaru of casting a spell over him. As they returned to land Maui planned his revenge. When the canoe landed Maui knocked his brother-in-law down and pinned Irawaru under the outrigger. Maui jumped all over Irawaru's back until he stretched it out. Irawaru's legs grew shorter, he grew a tail and long fur appeared all over his body. Maui then grabbed his face and pulled it out. Thus Maui had created the first Maori dog. Of course, Maui's sister wasn't too thrilled about it!

Since then many ancestors have had pet dogs. One in particular was Paoa, the captain of Horouta. He had a much-loved pet dog called Whakao. One day as they explored the bush the dog got lost and by nightfall had still not been found. That night the dog was heard whimpering in the bush. The next morning Paoa found his dog. He named that particular piece of bush Pipiwhakao (Whimpering Whakao). Just to the south near Te Muriwai is a cliff face called Te Kuri-a-Paoa. (The dog of Paoa).

White Heron

The white heron is a prince in the world of light yet is very shy so is rarely seen. Maori honour the white heron in their folklore and proverbs. Chiefs of the highest rank were likened to the beautiful white bird. One of the most famous Maori proverbs states emphatically 'He kotuku rerengatahi' — The white heron flies alone. Basically it suggests the white heron is so rare and so precious it has no peer. It also alludes to the chiefly attributes of leadership and direction.

Maori believe that decisiveness is an admirable quality. As a result white heron plumes were highly prized by our leaders. These plumes were often worn by people of high rank to show they had status and power. The expression 'Te Rau-o-Titapu' (The plume of Titapu) is sometimes used to describe those of rank. Titapu was actually a warrior of note who lived in the east. One day his brother-in-law ambushed him near a swamp and Titapu was killed. When he descended to the land of darkness he magically change himself into a proud white heron — some say because the heron had witnessed the murder. Titapu then flew back to the world of light to seek his revenge. He found his murderer and stabbed him to death. Thus Titapu is forever linked with the kotuku.

Maui has similar links to the famous white bird. It was Maui who discovered Te Ara Whaiti-a-Maui (The narrow path of Maui). Maori know this as the path to the underworld, home of Hinenui-te-po. The proud white heron carries the souls along this path to the river of the underworld down in Rarohenga. Maori know this as a very special place called Te Muriwaihou and it is the first stage of the souls' journey to the world of darkness. The birds leave the souls there to be cleansed and prepared for the next stage. And thus … it is the kotuku who delivers our souls to Hinenui-te-po.

Kaka

The boisterous, cheeky kaka has always been a favourite family member. When the Maori settlers first arrived the forests were buzzing with life. The kaka, kakariki, korimako, tui and kakapo all thrived in the lush forests of Aotearoa. Maori hunted many birds for food including the kaka. Its meat was tasty and the feathers were used to make cloaks. Some birds were kept as pets and were taught to speak or recite karakia.

Long ago deep in the forests Kaka came upon his little friend Kakariki. Kaka noticed the bright red feathers on Kakariki's chest and spoke.

'Foolish bird,' he said. 'You should hide your bright red feathers.'

'Why should I hide them?' asked Kakariki. 'They are red like the blood of Tawhaki; everyone admires them.'

'You think so?' said Kaka. 'When Tane gave me my brown feathers it was to honour Papatuanuku. It is easier to hide as well. That shows he loves me best as I am able to catch more insects and thrive,' said Kaka. 'With those bright feathers you can be seen for miles,' he continued.

'But Tane has clothed me in green like the forest and red like the sunset — surely that proves his love for me,' sang Kakariki.

'Silly bird,' cried Kaka. 'You think Tane would give you gaudy feathers if he really loved you? No, my little friend, those feathers are not signs of Tane's love.'

Kakariki was distraught. 'What shall I do?' he asked.

'Fear not, little friend,' said Kaka. 'Give them to me and I will hide them beneath my wings.'

So Kakariki gave Kaka his brilliant red feathers. Kaka attached them to his wings then soared high into the sky. Immediately Kakariki noticed how beautiful the feathers were and realised he had been tricked by the cunning Kaka.

Woodpigeon

Of all our family members Kereru (wood pigeon) is probably the vainest. Kereru spends most of his time grooming himself and just loves to show off his brilliant coat. Like most birds kereru were hunted by the Maori. Not only did they eat the meat but they also adored the beautiful feathers.

Hina lost her husband and was so grief-stricken she threw herself into the sea. She eventually washed ashore and was found by two brothers who carried her to their village. When their chief Tinirau saw her he insisted she be his wife, despite her many protests.

Hina was not happy with Tinirau and longed for her family. Far away her brother Maui-mua was looking for her. As he searched for her it occurred to him to ask Rehua (the god of kindness) for help. Rehua lived on the tenth heaven. Maui-mua magically assumed the form of Rupe, a magic Kereru. Eventually he reached the house of Rehua. He was exhausted but Rehua revived him.

Rupe then asked Rehua about his sister. Rehua told him she was living on Motutapu (Sacred Island). Rupe flew down the heavens and straight to Motutapu. There he perched in a window to look for Hina. People began throwing stones and spears to catch the pigeon. Rupe avoided them. This continued for some time and people believed the pigeon had bewitched their village. Soon everyone was there to see the magic pigeon they called Rupe.

When Rupe saw his sister he called, 'It is Hina, Hina who was lost.' She recognised his voice. Rupe took her hand and they flew off together to live with Rehua on the tenth heaven.

There Rupe became the keeper of Rehua's house, where he set up the post on the tenth heaven where Kaitangata (the man-eater) was killed. It is Kaitangata's blood that stains the sky red at sunset, reminding us of Rupe.

Also by Warren Pohatu

available in English and Māori